# Healing Is a Gift

Also by Alexandra Vasiliu

*Healing Words*

*Time to Heal*

*Dare to Let Go*

*Be My Moon*

*Blooming*

*Magnetic*

*Plant Hope*

*Through the Heart's Eyes*

# Healing Is a Gift
Poems for Those Who Need to Grow

Alexandra Vasiliu

Stairway Books
Boston

*Healing Is a Gift: Poems for Those Who Need to Grow* by Alexandra
Vasiliu. Boston, Stairway Books, 2021

Editing services provided by Melanie Underwood at
www.melanieunderwood.co.uk
Cover Illustrations: Ngupakarti via www.shutterstock.com
Book Illustrations: Singleline via www.shutterstock.com

ISBN-13: 9798496041645

*To all those who need*
*to heal, grow, and live meaningfully*

# Contents

Alexandra Vasiliu

# Healing Is a Gift

## The Greatest Gift

Dear woman,
stop showering yourself
with expensive and useless presents
only to cover your heart's wounds
and to hide yourself
from your essential problems.
Nothing external
or artificial will help you.
You need to turn inwards.
You need to face your heart.
Your wounds.
Your troubles.
Your turmoil.
Look inside yourself.
Run to your inner screaming self.
Stop smothering its voice
with useless presents.
Stop the crazy hunting of cheap gifts.
Take care of your heart.
Take care of your little pearl.

Heal your precious inner self.
Heal yourself with gentleness
and patience.
Trust me,
healing your scarred heart
is the greatest gift
that you can ever give to yourself.
And this is what you need to do
from now on.
Work on the greatest gift
you can ever give
to your inner, precious self.
Start mending your heart.

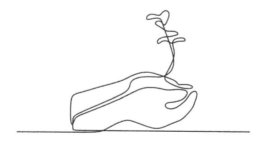

## Don't Train Yourself

Don't train yourself to avoid suffering
in life.
It is a hilarious attempt.
Nobody could ever get rid of pain.
Nobody could ever avoid drinking
from the bitter river of afflictions.
Nobody.
What you can do instead,
is to prepare yourself
to be emotionally mature,
wise
and strong,
so life's punches do not hit you
straight in the face
and knock you down.
Prepare yourself
to cope with pain,
disappointment,
suffering,
depression,

and loneliness.
Prepare yourself for tough times.
Train your heart to be brave,
so you can drink
from the bitter river of afflictions
with great fortitude.

## Swim as Hard as You Can

If you are heartbroken,
tears can drift you away
from what is important to you now.
Your healing.
Don't despair.
Stop crying.
All the tears in the world
can't solve anything.
Stop crying.
You fill up the holes in your heart
with tears,
and you might create
an ocean of sadness
around you.
A vast ocean.
And your condition will not change.
Take a deep breath.
There is no greater danger
right now
than your despair.

Remind yourself,
you are not meant
to spend your life adrift
in an ocean of pain.
Take a deep breath
and try to collect your thoughts.
I know
that you already ask yourself
how you can move on
with your life,
how can you ever feel whole again
since sadness surrounds you
and fear lingers in the air.
Don't despair.
Your pain is temporary.
Accept everything that happened.
I know you are scarred,
that your heart is a mess now,
but your heart is everything
you have been left with.
Try to gather courage and strength,
and dive into the dark ocean
that surrounds you –
your pain.
And swim.
Swim as hard as you can.
You have to conquer everything

that belonged to you.
You have to be whole again.
Swim.
Swim as hard as you can.
You must conquer your world again.
You are already very strong.
The raging waves are your feelings,
the endless sky is full of your grief,
and everything in between is your life.
Your actual life.
Swim.
Swim as hard as you can.
This is the only way
you can change your pain into hope.
One day,
you will find yourself
across the other side of this dark ocean.
One day,
you will realize
that your strength came out of
your despair.
And you will embrace your heroic heart
under the inner sky of peace.

## No Permission Needed

Don't live stuck inside your ivory tower
babysitting your insecurities
or unconsciously nurturing your trauma.
Break your heart's door,
get out of your comfort zone,
be proactive,
and allow your feelings to have a voice.
Seagulls never ask for permission
to scream.
Blue jays never ask for permission
to sing.
Your heart needs a voice too.
Let her say what she needs to say.
If there is no one to listen,
let your heart speak with the sky.
If you can't speak,
sing,
write
or draw.
Just let your feelings have a voice.

Seagulls never ask for permission
to scream
or fly.
So neither do you.
Get out of your ivory tower,
involve yourself intentionally
in your healing process,
hope,
pray,
rise,
be free,
and fly high.

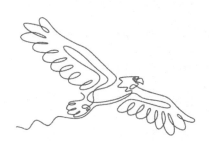

## Self-Love Starts Here

When someone breaks your heart
and millions of your soul's pieces
scatter all around you,
stay still for a moment,
touch the most painful point of your heart,
and say to yourself,
"I am going to be fine."
There is only one path
you should follow.
The path that leads you
to your precious inner self.
The path that rekindles
the connection with yourself.
And this is the path of self-acceptance.
The path of self-love.
The path of self-respect.
This is the path
you should traverse
to gather all your broken pieces.
This is the path

you need to walk
to mend yourself.
You can no longer afford
to be generous in love,
to the detriment of your feelings.
You need to find the balance
between being in love
and being wise,
love yourself more
and unlove toxic people.
You need to be emotionally mature.
You need to put yourself first.
You need to find a safe path
for your heart.
It is too expensive to waste yourself
on those who don't treasure you
or who throw your gems out
in the dark.

When someone breaks your heart
and everything inside you crumbles,
say to yourself,
"This is the goodbye time
to my younger self
who hasn't already learned
how to choose a mate
who never turns love into ashes.

"This is the right moment
when I must follow the path
to healthy self-love.
It might be a short sprint
or a lifelong marathon.
But self-love starts here and now
for me.
I need to learn
how to avoid going through
a breakup again.
I need to learn
how to choose a man
who never turns into a stranger.
I need to know
how to choose true love.
I need to be wise.
Self-love begins now."

## Such Bad Manners

Who could have ever imagined
that pain has such bad manners?
Pain never says "Hello."
She slams the door of your heart
and enters your feelings
in the blink of an eye.
Pain is rude.
She storms in
whenever she wants.
She destroys your peace
like a tornado that smashes everything.
She never asks you
if you have time to chat or not,
or if you have something to drink.
Pain sits down
in the middle of your heart,
she makes herself comfortable,
and devours your beautiful feelings
and thoughts.
She is the center of your attention,

while you become invisible.
She never treats you well.
You are only prey.
A victim.
Pain has this extraordinary power
to make you feel utterly alone
and irrelevant.
Pain is a thief of hearts.
She robs you of peace,
innocence,
and joy.
Pain has such bad manners.
But this behavior
should give you the courage
to grow wings
and soar high above it.
You should never share the same space
with pain.
Fight back
and fly away from her.

## Your Top Priority

One who doesn't take self-healing
as a top priority,
becomes a slave to the past,
to fear,
to pain,
and to anxiety.
Day by day,
the soul of this person loses any hope
in freedom.

## The Best Place

Never postpone your healing journey.
You will live in your soul
for the rest of your life.
Make this invisible place
as beautiful as a forest glade.
Work on your soul.
Nurture it with love.
Light it up with hope.
Heal its wounds and scars.
Build a wonderful haven,
so you will be delighted
to live in it
for the rest of your life.

## Be Present

You can never take a month off
from your heart's wounds.
You can never go on vacation
outside your heart.
Get rid of all these glittering promises
that make you think
you can escape from your sufferings.
Anywhere you go,
you will face your heart
with all its angels and demons.
So don't search for exotic destinations
to solve your internal problems.
Take a deep breath,
be present
in your heart,
and face all the hidden ghosts.
Be aware
that you have vulnerabilities,
weaknesses,
and imperfections.

Be aware
that you will always need
to work on your emotional health.
Be aware
that your heart is the most valuable asset
that you always carry with you.
Be aware
that your heart is a divine, unique gift.
Never treat it
like you could replace it.
Instead,
take your time
and heal your wounds.
Allow yourself to radiate love again.
You are a piece of heaven.

## The Right Place

Don't search for exotic destinations.
All the roads in the world will lead you
to your heart.
There is no escape.
Choose to go to the right place
from the very beginning.
Choose to be present in your heart.
Be aware of yourself.
Your company is invaluable.
Your heart is sacred,
as sacred as the pure smile of a child.
Work on making yourself a better soul –
it is a never-ending process.
Discover your inner abundance of beauty,
the gentlest parts of your soul,
your hidden rivers of love.
Be present in your heart.

Alexandra Vasiliu

## When Healing Starts

Healing starts
when you don't allow
a corruptible way of thinking
to creep again into your heart.
You assume
that your life has to change,
and for this,
you fight
with all your wisdom and might.

## Explore

While you heal,
you don't take inventory of
your inner wounds,
you don't count your tears,
you don't pile up your insecurities,
you don't create a competition
with your ideal self.
You explore your heart.
Self-reflection is an invisible tunnel
leading you to the depths of your heart.
You are an adventurous explorer.
You map the cave of your heart.
You face the stalactites
of your sufferings
and the potholes
of your breakups.
You are very brave
to go so deep inside yourself,
without help or a companion.
Please don't stop, my friend.

Keep exploring your heart.
Self-healing is a solitary trip,
yet let God infuse you with courage.

When you think you've reached
the bottom of your heart,
call out your feelings and greet them,
"Hi, love!
Hi, sadness!
Hi, kindness!
Hi, pain!
Hi, anger!
Hi, forgiveness!
Hi, hope!"

Then, talk to them,
"I have come so far
to speak with you.
I need you all to make peace with me.
I need you all to heal
because I want to live again.
Let's make peace.
Let's forgive one another.
Let's grow together
toward light.
Let's live in harmony.
I need a new, pure, beautiful heart."

Remember that you are the owner
of your heart.
You are the master of your feelings.
Don't let them chain you.
Talk to them.

This is a cathartic moment.
Your special moment.
Your healing time.
Speak with your feelings.
Talk to your heart.

Don't leave until you win, my friend.
You are the master of your heart.

## It Is Not Wrong

It is not wrong to be alone with yourself
from time to time.
It is not wrong to spend time
with your soul
and discover your deepest needs.
It is not wrong to get to know yourself,
your weaknesses,
your strengths.
It is not wrong to understand
that you might have unrealistic dreams
and impossible expectations.
It is not wrong to come to appreciate
your worth.
It is not wrong
to learn who you are,
what you want to be,
and what you never want to become.
It is not wrong to be alone
with yourself
to look inward,

and to find your true self.
It is not wrong to stop being attached
to an artificial image
created by society.
It is not wrong to take time
to speak with yourself.
It is not wrong
to work on
the most important long-term relationship
you will have
in your life –
the relationship with yourself.
Make a habit, my friend.
From time to time,
be alone with yourself,
spend time with your soul,
and talk with yourself.
At some point,
you will find a friend
in your soul.

## You Are More

You are more than your trauma.
You are more than
your millions and millions
of resentments,
tears,
sighs,
and never-ending nightmares.
You are more than your past.
Get rid of all these limiting beliefs
that keep you locked
in afflictions.
You are not the sum
of the painful words
that you keep saying to yourself.
You are not a collection
of devaluing messages
that you keep sending to your soul.
You are not a collection
of bad experiences
that you keep remembering.

You are something other than trauma
and heartbreak.
You are something else.
You are much more special than
you think.
You are much purer than
you accept.
Dare to look into the mirror of hope.
Dare to believe in yourself.
Dare to love yourself.
Dare to say to yourself,
"Even though I have traveled through
hell,
I am something else than
that deep darkness
that I faced.
Even if my soul is all wounded,
I am still a miracle,
a beautiful flower,
a glimmer of love,
a poem of courage.
I am still strong.
I am a miracle."

## A Promise

My dear soul,
I will steal the moon for you.
I will steal the sun
and the whole sky for you.
I will do all the impossible things
so you can heal.
I want you to believe
that there is nothing
more beautiful
in this world
than you,
my beautiful, precious soul.
Even if you are sad,
you are still magnificent.
You are glistening like the moon.
You are spreading kindness
like the sun spreads warmth.
You are infinite and immortal
as is the sky.
You are beautiful and precious.

Your worth is beyond your trauma.
Believe me,
you are beautiful.
I pray
that one day,
you will shine again.
But for now,
please start healing yourself.
Even if it is going to take time,
I will stand by you.
I know
that healing is not a *hocus-pocus* trick,
so don't rush.
I will be here.
Never doubt that.
My dear soul,
I will keep loving you
and do all the impossible things,
so you can see your worth,
your beauty,
your innate potential.
I will be here,
and help you heal.
I love you,
and love is my gift for you.

## Wash Your Heart

When you heal your broken heart,
you will go through
a purification process,
an ongoing cleansing experience.
Don't be afraid.

Has anybody told you
that all heartbreaks are dirty?
Has anybody said to you
that each pain tastes like mud?
Don't be scared.
Wash your heart's wounds.
Cleanse your injuries with hope.

Self-love should be a way of life,
a simple way to keep yourself pure.
Water your scars with love.
Has anybody told you
that love is in your DNA,
connected to the purpose of your life?

Has anybody told you
that healing is all about love
and love is all about healing?
Has anybody told you
that both statements are true and sacred?

Love and healing are more than
just feelings;
they are dynamic acts of courage
toward yourself,
and wonderful daily practices
toward all around you.

Healing and self-love are
compassionate ways
of regaining your dignity and purity.

Don't be afraid.
Be intentional with your heart.
Wash your wounds, my dear.
Accept yourself.
Make a commitment
to accept your imperfections
every day.
See yourself
through the unfiltered lens of love.
Your worth is uncountable.

One day,
you will find yourself
pure and precious
as a piece of gold.
One day,
you will see yourself
as I already see you now.
One day,
you will appreciate your authenticity.
One day,
beyond elation,
you will feel welcomed again
in your heart.

## Your Golden Trophy

If you don't heal
your heart's wounds,
you will end up collecting insecurities,
sufferings,
and unshed tears.
You will become a hoarder
who stores toxic sentiments.
Your painful experiences will pile up
inside your heart.
How will you live
with all this emotional stuff
suffocating you?
If you don't throw away
your bad memories,
your everyday life will become impeded.
It would be best
if you start changing yourself.
Start letting go.
Step by step.
Start with a tear.

Tomorrow move to something else.
Let go of a cruel word
that someone told you
a long time ago.
Erase that painful word
from your heart.
Water your scar with affection.
Drop a seed of kindness
in your wound.
Forgive that person.
Let grace take roots in your heart.
Hope will rise after letting go.
Then, do more.
Throw away your harrowing experiences.
Little by little.
Start with the less difficult ones.
You will notice
how brave you are.
A glimmer of hope will start shining
in your inner depths.
Keep working on your heart, my friend.
Overcome your anxieties.
Open the door of your heart
in the middle of the night,
and face your ghosts.
Who dares to scare you?
Speak up loud with your biggest fear.

"Why do you terrorize me?
Why do you want to control me?
I will not be your servant."

Stay busy healing your heart, my friend.
Remember that all the pain
that is not healed yet
keeps you locked
and weighs you down,
and all the pain that is healed
is your golden trophy,
because you rose, fought, and won.

## Change from the Inside Out

Don't spend money
buying new shoes
or replacing your old clothing
with trendy things.

Don't spend money
dying your hair
or trying to look different.

Don't waste money on things
that your soul can't savor.
Your turmoil will be the same.
Your problems will remain unchanged.

Don't fool yourself.

Have the guts
to change yourself
from the inside out
and wrestle with your emotional issues.

Become kind,
and you will always look beautiful.

Stay generous,
and you will always be joyful.

Be honest,
and you will always be peaceful.

Be meek and humble,
and you will always be
like milk and honey
for all your friends.

## The Healthy Self-Love

If you ever want to abandon yourself,
try to remember my words:
"Don't leave yourself.
Right now,
your soul is like a baby
in the middle of a storm.
You must protect it.
Hold your soul with the arms of love.
Don't abandon your baby.
Healthy self-love comes from
understanding.
Healthy self-love comes from maturity.
Healthy self-love comes from
inner strength.
Go inside the storm,
fight, and save your soul.
Your baby needs a warm home.
What else could be a warmer home
than your true, healthy,
unconditional self-love?"

## The Best Birthday Message

When I turned eighteen,
I received the best birthday message
I ever got.
In vain, I tried to figure out
who the sender was,
I could never find out.
The message was simple,
"I pray
you will find the safest path
to love yourself more."

I closed my eyes
and inscribed those words
on my heart.
In time
I realized
that self-love is the most useful gift
I can give to myself.

## Learning to Love

Recovering from emotional wounds
is the most challenging process of all.
No convalescence runs on for so long.
No rehabilitation lasts so long.
No, nobody told you
that healing your emotional wounds is
a lifelong journey.
It takes a lifetime
to heal your hidden wounds,
and learn to love again
in a healthy way.
Oh, my friend,
it takes a lifetime
to realize that healing is all about love,
and love is only a gift.
The most beautiful gift.
Give this gift to your inner child.

## Hope

When everything around you
is falling apart,
remind yourself
that Hope is a magical place
where all implausible dreams
stop being impossible,
where all good powers
belong naturally to you,
where love,
self-confidence,
and peace
call your name out loud.

When everything around you
is falling apart,
remind yourself
that you can find refuge
in Hope,
in that magical,
invisible place

where you can go without a car
or a passport.

When everything around you
is falling apart,
remind yourself
that for moving on,
all you need is Hope.

And Hope is the name of a pure heart.

## Make a Promise

When pain bites your heart,
make a promise,
"Today,
I want to be positive
with each person
I encounter."
And the snake of pain will slither away.

When depression swallows
small pieces of your heart,
make a promise,
"Today,
I want to create something beautiful.
A poem.
A song.
A cake.
Or at least,
I will make a baby smile at me.
Today,
I will create something beautiful

in this world.
"I will not go down the road of
depression.
I will not let myself be fooled.
I will not fall into the trap of depression."
And the monster of depression will pop
like a balloon.

When dark thoughts grind your heart,
make a promise,
"Today,
I want to be kind to myself.
I will make a hot cocoa
and stay late in bed.
I will listen to a concert.
I will read a meaningful book.
I will start writing in a daily journal.
I will take a walk in a park.
I will admire all the little kids
playing without worries.
I will take their smiles with me
like some invisible Band-Aids.
My heart will need them.
I will say a prayer
all the way back home.
I will say it over and over again
until my heart rises from the ashes.

"I will think of all the people
who helped me overcome
my life's obstacles.
I will say *thank you* to them.
Maybe gratitude can take
the shape of a bird
and fly quickly to them.
On my way home,
I will buy two bunches of tulips:
one for me
and one for my old neighbor.
Who can reject a symbol of innocence?
Today,
I will be kind to myself.
I will surround myself with positivity,
peace,
patience,
love, and beauty.
Today,
I will be kind to myself.
I will not make room for dark thoughts.
I will be meek and kind."

And the vampire of dark thoughts
will vanish
like a fictional character
from a sad story.

## Waiting for You

Trauma is a foreign country.
Nothing speaks to your heart,
and you can understand nothing.
Every morning,
when you wake up,
you feel weird.
"What am I going to do here?
I am a foreigner
in the middle of a nightmare."
Trauma makes you feel
like you have been sent into exile –
outside your heart,
far from your comfort zone,
far from your pure dreams,
far from your hopes.
My friend,
you must prepare your luggage
and come back home.
Maybe it will take some time for you.
Only God knows

how long your journey will be.
But you can no longer live
in your trauma.
Leave that painful country.
You can't spend the rest of your life
in suffering,
depression,
reproaches,
and anxiety.
Come back home!
Come back to your beautiful heart.
You will travel a lot
and pass through *The Healing Lands*.
You will walk barefoot
like an ancient pilgrim
who believed in self-restoration.
But eventually, you will be home again.
And what is home
if not a peaceful heart?
Come back home, my friend.
You have been hurt for so long.
You have been gone in exile
for so long.
Come back home.
Nothing is sweeter than home.
Come back.
Your pure heart is waiting for you.

## Nobody Told Me

Nobody told me
that each heartbreak smells like dirt.
Nobody whispered in my ear,
"You will feel so unclean,
so muddy,
so messy,
so small
that you will spend
hours and hours
under the shower.
You will rub and scrub your skin
frenetically,
trying to dissolve
the pain from your heart.
You will take a shower
so many times a day,
just to wash away the feeling
of being rejected."
Nobody told me
how much I will need to cleanse

and renew my soul
after a heartbreak.
Nobody told me
that each heartbreak would mire me
in mud
over and over again.
Nobody told me
the price I had to pay to rebuild myself.
I had to find out the truth the hard way.
So here I am,
my friend,
in front of you,
telling you to be brave and patient.
Keep cleansing and healing
your broken heart,
wash your wounds,
wipe out all the cruel words,
clean out your inner debris,
and declutter your soul.
You have so much beauty underneath.
You have poems
hidden
in every wrinkle of your scars.
Just be patient
and keep cleansing and healing your soul.
One day,
you will regain your pure heart.

And a pure heart, my friend, is a triumph
in this world
of lies,
betrayals,
breakups,
cruelty,
dishonesty,
delusion,
revenge,
and hate.
A pure heart is a treasure.
A unique pearl.
A pearl of love,
patience,
and wisdom.
You must protect it.
And right now,
in the depths of your trauma,
something amazing happens,
something that you are not aware of.
Your tears cleanse your wounds.
Your tears add layers of peace
to your heart.
Drop after drop,
your tears create a miracle –
they form a little pearl.
You are renewed.

And one day,
in this world
of lies,
betrayals,
breakups,
cruelty,
dishonesty,
delusion,
revenge,
and hate,
you will be able to reveal your rare gem.
One day,
your heart will shine again.
One day,
your heart will be healed
and never feel
dirty,
muddy,
messy,
or small
again.
One day,
your heart will be ready to love,
yet she will choose someone
who appreciates
the value of a real pearl.
One day, my friend...

## A Special Dream

Last night,
I had a dream.
We were walking hand in hand
in a mysterious forest.
One moment,
I asked you,
"My darling,
I hope
you will never hurt me.
My heart is like a battlefield,
covered with dead dreams,
bloody hopes, and buried love words."
You touched my lips with your finger.
"*Shh*!
I will never harm you.
Fear not, my love.
A heart like yours needs a crown."
And then,
in a blink of an eye,
the forest changed into light.

## You Kept Your Armor On

You have never shown me your heart.
You have kept your armor on
and let me think
you were a brave knight,
yet you were just a scared wanderer,
followed by a devoted, dark dog –
your depression.
I tried to save you,
but your dog always smelled your scent
and shadowed you.
Sometimes,
it seemed to me
that the roles changed,
and you were the poor dog,
with no will,
and your depression was your master.
In the end,
you left me
saying
you were not ready for love.

You chose your dog.
I left you a note,
"You are never too old
to start healing your thoughts.
I hope
one day
your heart will fit
inside my words."

# When You Left Me

I was born
on the day you left me.
I was born
on the day
you slammed the door
behind you,
leaving me
alone,
scared,
and confused
in a chaotic world.
I was born
on the staircase
you were running down
away from me.
I was born
in the dust
that your footsteps lifted up
in the air.
I was born

in the darkness
that your last words created.
I was born
on that unforgettable day
you rejected and abandoned me.
Oh, how much I remember that day!
You never turned your head back.
You kept walking away from me,
believing
that everything you said and did
was right and fair.
I couldn't take my eyes off you.
Your body was straight
like a foolish exclamation point
in a world of questions and commas.
You were sure
about what you said and did.
I stared at you
for a few minutes more.
The faster you walked away,
the quicker you looked like
anybody else.
A common person.
Before making a turn
at the corner of the street,
I noticed
that you stopped carrying a heart

in your chest.
It was so strange.
You had nothing inside yourself.
You were just an empty body.
A man without a heart –
that was you.

And then,
in that very moment,
I heard a scream.
It was so strange.
It was me –
I screamed.
I was born.
Oh, God,
I was born.

Tears covered my skin.
I kept my eyes wide open
for the whole day.
I hoped
you would return and see me.
But you have never returned.
By the end of that day,
my eyes became bigger and bigger
like two bleeding wounds.
How was I supposed to survive?
Nobody asked me anything.
I was just a tiny newborn,
thrown into a world of loneliness.
I was a newborn
fed with the milk of pain
and covered with the blanket of rejection.
I was born
on that unforgettable day
when you left me.
And since then,
I have had nothing else to do
than figure out
how to outgrow my trauma.

## The Sixth Sense

People say that there are five senses.
Then, how is it possible
to smell, hear, touch, and taste,
and still feel dead inside?
There must be a sixth sense
that gets damaged
when someone breaks your heart.
My friend,
take care of your soul,
and allow yourself
to see, smell, hear, touch, and taste
with your secret sense.
Only the sixth sense will help you grow
your most authentic self.
Only this sense will make you feel alive.

## Scribble This Message

If you feel broken inside
like a bird without feathers and wings,
please dig deeper into your heart
and scribble this message,
"You are not your pain.
You are not your sadness.
You are not your flaws.
You are something else.
You are a miracle
waiting to be discovered.
You are only poetry
waiting for a caring soul
to whisper it
all life long."

## Dear Heart

Dear heart,
I promise
that from this day on,
I will always protect you,
heal you,
understand you,
and help you grow.
I hope
one day,
you will say to me,
"Thank you for not leaving me.
Thank you for loving me."
I know
that sometimes,
self-love is an act of bravery,
so from this day on,
I want to be bold, brave, heroic.
For you.
Only for you, my dear heart.

## Don't Beg

Dear woman,
if you want to heal your broken heart,
you must begin a new life,
with new thoughts,
and a new heart.
Start your healing journey
with my friendly reminder,
"Don't beg for love.
Love always comes as a gift."

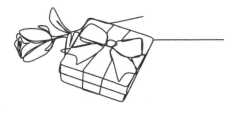

## Invite God

When you decide to heal your wounds,
invite God to assist and support you.
Add grace to your healing story.
There are tiny places
in your vulnerable heart
where only his gentle hands can reach.
Healing your broken heart
will remind you of your human frailty
and your dependence on God.

## Healing Is a Gift

When someone breaks your heart,
you will need an anchor
to heal your inner wounds.
What could that anchor be?
You don't see anything around you.
You feel dead inside,
frozen in time,
connected to life
by a thread –
your daily routine.
Take heart, my dear,
surviving is not the best solution.
Peel away the layers of your pain,
look straight at your wounds,
and accept my words
as a strong anchor.
"There is no turning back.
You can't go back
into your past.
There is only a straight path ahead

calling on you –
the pathway of your healing.
"Walk on it.
Healing your heart's wounds
is the greatest gift
that you can ever give to yourself.

Be brave
and go only straight ahead
toward your new life."

## Time for Reflection

Sit down on the edge of your wounds,
delve into the abyss of your suffering,
and start talking to your pain.
There must be an answer
deeply buried
inside your heart.
There must be a healing hope
hidden
somewhere there.
Take your time
and discover what can save you.
Self-care needs resilience.
When you find this answer,
pull it out from your depths.
It will soothe your soul.

## Cry

Let your tears stream down your face.
They are seeds for your healing.
Let them drop
on the soil of your soul.
Let them take roots.
Let them change you.
Let them grow
as willow trees.
Every tear is a seed
for your metamorphosis.
Every tear is a reminder of
what you want to become.
Cry
if you feel this need.
One day,
all your tears will disappear,
and your heart will be a garden
full of flowers.
The flowers of wisdom.

## No Less Precious

If someone hurts you,
remind yourself
that you are no less precious than before.
You have only met
a person who couldn't hold a diamond –
your heart –
without breaking it.
What a poor soul!
Next time,
be the first who properly holds
the diamond of your heart.
You are a jewel.
Love starts with yourself.

## Like the Wind

If I could change my shape,
I would want to be like the wind.
I would have an invisible soul
encapsulated in an invisible body.
Tell me,
is there anyone
who could hurt the wind?
No.
Neither me nor you.
Don't smile.
Nobody can hurt the wind.
There are days
when I heal only with this thought.

## Don't Validate

If you avoid healing your heart's wounds,
you revalidate your trauma.
You run from your problems.
You play hide-and-seek
with your afflictions,
acting like a victim of your past.
You hide yourself in work,
proving to others that you are busy
and don't have time
to work on your emotional health.
These are simply justifications.
You keep pretending that you are okay.
Take a deep breath,
look at your broken heart –
you are not okay.
Stop pretending
your heart is not a chaotic place.
Stop pretending you are fine.
Stop running away from yourself.
If you need to weep or scream,

just go out and do it.
Make time for yourself.
Make time for your healing.
Look in the eyes of your wounds.
You can cope with that pain.
You are already strong.
Take another deep breath
and make a promise to yourself,
"Every day
I will dedicate time
to work on my emotional health.
I will find time for myself.
Every day
I will talk with my soul
like I would speak with an old friend.
Every day
I will plant a seed of hope and beauty
in my heart's wounds.
Every day
I will do something meaningful
for my soul.
Every day
I will be present in my heart."
Be brave and patient.
Go beyond
what you already know about yourself.
And you will heal.

## Meanings

When I endured loss,
I asked myself
if there could be a meaning in that.
I discovered
how fragile and vulnerable I was.
I discovered
that I had never been in control
of what truly mattered –
love.
I discovered
so many parts in my soul
that could never be healed again.
Now I know
that these parts of my soul
will remain forever silent
like old photographs.
Every day,
they will remind me
that I don't have to understand everything
in life.

I don't have to think
that everything must make sense
in the end.
Only God has all the answers.
Only God knows
the meaning of my loss
and any loss
in the world.
Moreover,
every day,
these parts of my soul
will remind me
that loss is a mystery
and like any mystery,
my loss is a sign of love.
"Dear heart,
stay humble
and act with more kindness,"
I say to myself
every time
I feel the ache of my pain again.
"This is all I can tell you
from now on.
Stay humble
and be kind."

## More Kindness

Don't treat your problems
as unnecessary complications,
but as a continuous training
to gain
more kindness.
If suffering doesn't make you kinder,
then what else in this world will?

## Be Fluent

No matter how many people harmed you,
try to become fluent in kindness.
Speak in this sweet, beautiful language,
and you will show
to yourself
and to everybody else
that you learned something essential
from your sufferings.
You will proclaim
that pain hasn't had the last word
and love has the power
to overcome any cruelty.
You will reveal your human dignity.
Pain couldn't turn you into a tiger.
Speak in kindness.
You have a noble heart –
a river of love,
compassion,
and hope.
Every time you speak in kindness,

you manifest your soft heart
that pain couldn't defeat.
Speak in kindness
every day.
Speak with yourself,
speak with others.
Just speak in kindness.
Healing always comes on the soft wings
of peace
and kindness.

## A Choice

My mom told me,
"Healing is a choice,
as well as kindness.
Be kind to yourself
and start healing your soul.
Healing and kindness are
the most beautiful gifts
that you can give to yourself
and to those around you.
These are the greatest gifts
that just keep on giving."
I remember her words
every morning and night.
What a solid reminder
to never give up
to become a beautiful soul
in this world!

## Far Away

Have you noticed
how far away you are from yourself?
You need to scream,
so your soul can hear
what you have to say.
There is an abyss inside you.
An abyss
that is getting wider
and wider
as days pass.
Have you noticed
the huge distance
between you and your soul?
You need daily reminders
to start building a bridge
toward your soul.
Have you noticed
how lonely you are
without your true self by your side?
You feel disconnected from yourself,

yet there is no better way
to return to yourself
than facing your problems.
Stop hiding from yourself.
All your troubles and traumas
are parts of your journey,
they are chapters in your life story.
Don't remain stubbornly faithful to them.
Be busy healing yourself,
get to the roots of your sadness,
and work on a real change.
Don't expect an overnight transformation.
Rekindling the connections
with your heart
takes time and strength.
You will need both.
Make time for yourself every day,
and find inspiration in good, gentle people
who encourage and support you.
Take their kind, healing words
into your heart,
and let them empower you.
Fight and rise.
Slowly, slowly
you will start wishing to have
a closer relationship with yourself.
You will start craving peace.

My friend,
rise above your misfortunes.
Fight for yourself.
Thus, there is nothing more remarkable
and more satisfying than
the journey of returning to yourself.
The journey of learning
self-love,
honesty,
kindness,
self-acceptance,
and courage.
Come back to yourself –
this is the gift
that you deserve.

## My Trace of Love

There were days
when I was sitting all alone
in my room.
I used to remember
all my past and faults.
I cried for hours.
Sometimes,
I wondered,
"How is it possible
for a heart
to store so much suffering?"
I raised my head
and looked through the window
to the farthest point on the horizon.
If I die tonight,
I wish
I could have loved more.
I wish
I could have been a living love poem
in all my life's contexts.

At least,
my trace of love
would have had an impact
on someone.
I would have never lived in vain,
I thought.
Then,
a glimmer of hope ignited my heart,
"Your time hasn't come to an end.
You must fight to rise again,
to heal your hidden wounds,
to gather wisdom,
to live
and love with all your heart.
Your time hasn't come to an end."

## I Am Not *Atlas*

"I am not *Atlas*,"
I said to myself this morning.
"The world does not rest
on my shoulders,
yet I don't know
what burden weighs me down."
Then,
I touched my chest
and felt a load heavier than
the entire universe.
"This is your broken heart,"
I heard a voice
inside my chest.

Tears came to my eyes
and made me promise,
"Oh, dear heart,
I will do everything I can
to help you heal.
I will change myself
from a soul of dust
into a soul of light.
I will help you return
to innocence
and beauty.
I will help you become
as light as a feather.
I will help you heal
and enrich your life.
I will help you be happy again."

**Five Words**

Embed my words into your heart,
"Hope rises after letting go,"
and remember them
whenever you face difficulties.
Repeat these words
as often as you need them.
They will help you become self-aware
and avoid falling again into
the toxic patterns of your life.
They will help you find
the true path
to light.

## I Will Rise

When your heart aches so badly
and you see nothing around you
but darkness,
your time for rising has come.
I know
you hide a raging, black ocean
inside your heart,
yet you can't continue like this –
you have already hit bottom.
You reached a dead end in your life.
Stop walking with your head down.
Stop weeping over nothing.
Stop blaming yourself for everything,
including the fact that you exist.
Get up
and water your heart
with fresh hope,
"Life has many unveiled, joyful surprises,
and some of them are waiting for me."
Get up.

In the name of love and hope,
you must rise like a phoenix
and reinvent yourself.
Get up.
Everybody needs a second chance,
so give that second chance
to your inner self.
In the name of love,
in the name of hope,
in the name of beauty,
in the name of life,
say to yourself,
"From this day on,
I will rise.
And I will do nothing other
than rise
and rise
and rise."

## The Only Change

The only change
that matters
in life
is the personal transformation.
Don't spend time
trying to change the world.
Change yourself.
Shift your mindset.
Invest time and attention
into growing
and becoming a healing soul.
This is the reason
why you are here on earth.

## A Phoenix

As long as you hope,
you are a phoenix
that fights for her rebirth.
You want a second chance.
The best second chance.

As long as you heal yourself,
you are a phoenix
that fights for her renewal.
You wish to rise from ashes.
The ashes of your past.

As long as you pray,
you are a phoenix
that fights to soar again
high
in the sky.
The sky of your life.

## Recreation

Healing is a tremendous act of recreation.
You rebuild yourself.
Be patient.
It takes time to recreate
a pure heart.
Don't let anyone kill your enthusiasm
with cruel words.
You need to rise.
Healing leads you to inner strength.

## Best Healing Practices

Every day,
stick to your best healing practices.
Every day,
make time for reflection
and introspection.
Every day,
investigate your heart
and its emotional needs.
Every day,
do something beneficial
for your mental and emotional health.
Start filling a journal.
Buy flowers
and plant them in your backyard.
Treat with ice cream
all your little neighbors.
Order a beautiful blouse
and offer it
to someone who needs it.
Spread joy.

If you run out of ideas,
at least say a little prayer.
A prayer for yourself,
a prayer for your loved ones,
a prayer for the world.
Spread love through your thoughts.
Every day,
continue becoming a better person,
a healing soul
in this sick society.
Spend every day of your life
planting
seeds of love and wisdom
here and there.
First,
in your heart's wounds.
And then,
in the hearts of those around you.
Spend your lifetime changing yourself.
Stick to your best healing practices.
Be a light.
One day,
you will shine.

## A Healing Dream

Last night
I had a dream.
A young man told me,
"I hope the moon fits in your heart.
In the middle of the night,
I will find the sky
in your arms."
I woke up
and stopped feeling alone.
Somewhere in this world,
there must be a man waiting for me.
A man with poems in his heart.
A man who sends me dreams.
A man that can heal me
with his love.

## Where Are Those Keys?

There were days in my life
when I drowned in loneliness
and had a strong feeling of estrangement.
My life was a depressing place for me.
I felt like a lost expat.
I roamed the city streets for hours.
I checked my phone
and browsed my list of contacts
several times a day,
yet I couldn't find a friend to call.
I raised my hand toward the sky
and wrote my hope in the clouds,
"I want a warm home.
I want to find the keys to my heart.
I want to go inside myself
and feel welcome again.
I want to find a friend in myself.
Where are the keys to my heart?
Who has seen them?"

## My Home

Healing is my home.
I know that.
My heart loves to live
in this haven of love,
clarity,
and hope.
In a world of wars and hate,
healing is my home.

## Overcoming Depression

Nobody knew about my battles
with depression.
Nobody knew
how much I fought
in the depths of my heart.
Nobody knew
that each tear added
a new layer of sadness.
Nobody knew
how much I wanted
to see a shimmer of light.
I never thought
that so much pain could fit
inside my little heart.
There were days
when I didn't talk with anyone.
The words
I wished I could say,
were dead
on my lips.

All my hopes crawled into hibernation.
My heart was dissolved in sadness.

But one day,
I said to myself,
"I can't continue living
at the bottom of this ocean.
I have to come out.
I am drowned in darkness and depression.
I have become what I think.
I have to come out of my depression.
I am at my limit,
yet I know
and I believe
that my heart is precious
and has beautiful things to offer.
"I must fight constructively for my heart.

"I harmed myself too much.
It is time to heal
and believe in myself.
Depression can't define me.
I am the only one
who can define myself.
I have to fight.
One day,
I will look back
and say,
*I overcame depression.*
All my victories cost me tears.
Drop by drop,
hour after hour,
day after day.
I fought and fought,
but eventually,
I won.
I turned depression into true self-love."

## I Will Do My Best

At some point in your life,
make a promise to yourself,
"I will do my best
to never sink again
in depression,
to never allow anyone
to hurt me
and treat me mercilessly.
I will do my best
to never allow anyone
to consider me an object
without soul and feelings.
And I will allow myself to change,
to grow and bloom with hope,
to become free and strong.
I will do my best
to never go back to the self
I used to be."

## Get Up

Sometimes
you might fall back into the pattern
of your past bad practices.
Don't despair.
Don't say
that you can't change yourself.
Don't say
that you can make it out
of your inner chaos.
Get up
every time
you fall back into that pattern.
Get up
every time
you repeat doing something
that is toxic for your soul.
If it happens
a hundred times a day,
get up
a hundred times a day.

Stop counting your errors.
Just get up
and fight harder.
Every day
declutter your mind,
get rid of your dark thoughts,
and open up your heart to hope.
Every good thing is a labor of sacrifice,
so start getting rid of your toxic habits,
and build good healing practices
for your soul.

## Don't Be Ashamed

Don't be ashamed
if you still struggle with depression.
Don't permit dark thoughts
to dwell in your mind
and control you.
Don't blame yourself
if you search for shallow solutions.
You already know
that there is no fast route out
of depression.
Healing is laborious work.
It will take time
to exit this black forest of gloom.
Searching for light will not be
a thirty-minute event.
Don't be ashamed.
Don't blame yourself.
Just be bold, resilient, and patient.
Step by step,
you will learn

how to cope with your emotional turmoil
and how to strive to heal.
Just glue the cracks of your heart
and fill them up with self-acceptance.
Get out of your shell.
Search for a kind person
and learn something beautiful
from her emotional experience.
Lean on your best friend,
catch memorable sunrises together,
and buy flowers for each other.
Bring beauty back into your life.
Speak to God daily
and find out
what is your mission on this earth.
Look for a tiny glimmer in your heart
that can witness how wonderful you are.
Build noble goals for your life.
Make plans for the following summer.
Don't live caged in depression.
Thrive with hope
and let awe seep into your mind.
Healing is all about resilience.
You have both.
Put them to work
and start your inner revolution –
healing yourself from depression.

## The Image of Your Thoughts

Your mind is a battleground.
What kind of thoughts will win
your inner war?
Fight to have beautiful thoughts.
You will become the image
of your thoughts.
Moreover,
your life will reflect your thoughts.
Fight to gain a peaceful,
bright,
positive mindset.
You will always look beautiful.

## No Pills

You don't need pills
to overcome your heartbreak.
Gather courage
and say to yourself,
"I will never numb my pain.
I will face my suffering
no matter how deep it penetrates
my heart.
I will never camouflage my grief
with pills.
I will never sabotage myself.
I will not allow myself
to feel like an alien in my life.
I will do the best I can
to exit this hell
and never fall into it again.
I will heal myself with perseverance,
and I will rise from ashes.
I will reclaim
my strength, my purity, my worth.

"I will nurture my soul
with wisdom, faith, and self-love.
I will heal and rise again from ashes."
My friend,
stay strong.
You don't need pills
to heal after your heartbreak.
You don't need medications
to change yourself,
to become wise,
or to grow in a wholesome way.
You don't need pills
to use your intuition
and make good, loyal friends.
You don't need pills to let go,
move forward,
and live a life full of love.
Gather courage
and go through
this challenging life experience.
Fear not.
One day,
you will be healed
and look back with peace,
thinking how far you have come.
Be brave.
You don't need pills.

## A Glimmer of Hope

My mother once told me.
"Never empty your heart of hope.
Try to copy the moon
because on her lowest days,
a crescent moon starts to rise.
So, my darling,
imitate the moon,
never surrender,
hold on to a glimmer of hope,
and let your heart radiate
even a tiny ray of love.
You will find the strength
to go on."

## Don't Think

If someone tells you
that your pain will fade away in time,
don't judge this person.
Never think you are not understood.
Those words don't minimize
your suffering,
don't reject your feelings,
don't want to make you feel small.
Those words are meant to bridge
a painful silence.
Be patient, my friend.
Be patient with others.
Be patient with yourself.
Be patient with your pain.
Healing your heart's wounds takes time.
Healing is not a race
or a one-time quick choice.
Healing is a lifelong process.
Some flowers bloom quickly,
yet magnificent trees need time

to grow and fill the air
with their beautiful branches.
Be patient,
and when you ask yourself
where all this chaos ends,
remember my words:
"Let a seed teach you
how to grow amid tough times."
Healing your heart's wounds is
like a gardening process:
you seed hope,
pull out the weeds of pain,
and wait for love to grow again.
This is a painstaking labor of love.
But one day,
you will be able
to cross over many bridges
without support.
One day,
you will be able to admire
the beautiful flowers
that you seeded.
One day,
you will be able to forgive everybody,
including yourself.
And this will be the gist
of your healing process.

## Rebirth

Healing your heart's wounds is
so painful,
like giving birth
to a new version of yourself.
But you have to do it.
There is no other way to live
from now on.
You need a change.
Breathe in,
breathe out.
Give birth to a new self,
give love to your new self.
Transmit hope,
compassion,
and kindness
to your new self.
Breathe in,
breathe out.
Let go of the pain
you have been carrying

for so long,
and acknowledge this time
as a time of healing
and growth.
Breathe in,
breathe out.
Fill yourself with the wonder
of your rebirth.
Have you ever realized
how strong you really are?
Breathe in,
breathe out.
Giving birth to a new self
makes you experience
the true grace of God.
Breathe in,
breathe out.
Gather courage from this reality,
a beautiful butterfly comes from
an unattractive chrysalis.
Breathe in,
breathe out.
Let love infuse
every cell of your mind and soul.
Your rebirth is a fantastic work of art.

## Close Your Eyes

Close your eyes.
Remember the peaceful days
of your childhood
when the sun shone
in the summer afternoons.
You played without worries.
Nothing troubled you.
Try to embrace
the innocent child you were.
Go back to those blissful memories
and let your actual pains be melted away
under the warmth of your early life.
Step by step,
the cracks of your broken heart
will be filled
with a golden, healing light.
You will get back your confidence.
You will believe in yourself again.
Don't open your eyes yet.
Remember the peaceful days

of your childhood.
Walk barefoot again
in the grass
of your most beautiful memories.
Hold the hands of the child you were.
Can you believe
what a raw and beautiful soul you were?
The child you were
runs toward you now,
shouting,
"Don't give up.
A beautiful life is
for dreamers and fighters.
Be a dreamer
and dream of good things
becoming possible for you.
Be a fighter
and struggle
to make good things possible
for you."
Keep your eyes closed,
and let these words grow roots
in your heart.
I know
that life hasn't been easy for you,
but becoming a pure soul
is not easy either.

Look beyond
what you experience right now.
In the name of your childhood,
dare to heal,
to dream,
to fight,
and hope again.
The child you were
deserves a wonderful grown-up
to hug.

## Two Paths

Some people think
that you can be awakened by suffering,
but I have never believed
that this is the price I have to pay
to be spiritually aware of myself.
I chose the path of love.
My friend,
suffering is a complicated path.
Choose the simplest one
and the least disruptive –
stay meek, loving, kind, pure, honest,
and you will become aware
of your spiritual growth.
Keep your heart safe and innocent
as a child naturally does,
and you will become spiritually mature.
You don't need the sting of suffering
to touch the invisible skies of Love.

## Who Am I?

Each time you feel lost,
find the way back to your core
through my words.
"I am a poem.
A love poem
in a human body.
I am a song,
trying to find its way out
in the world.
A story.
A piece of stardust.
A pigeon,
looking for the quiet shore of joy.
I am an artwork in progress.
I am a complicated maze
of healing words,
hopes,
failures,
tears,
and love.

"I am a dream of love
wrapped in a human body.
I am a bold soul
going against the norm,
burning with hope,
and flying up high.
I am a poem.
A love poem
wishing
to be read by a poet."

## The Purification Process

If you feel burned to the ground,
I hope
you will find comfort in my words.
"Your heart is a piece of gold.
And as fire purifies gold,
you will also go through a painful process
to find out your true worth.
Accept this purification process.
There will be a time of incandescence,
cleansing,
forgiveness,
and rebirth.
Embrace this process of change.
In the end,
your heart will shine
like a diamond of love."

## Like a Doctor

When your heart is carrying
a heavy load of regrets,
say to yourself,
"Don't beat yourself up.
Harming yourself doesn't bring healing.
I wish
I could cure your pains
like a physician.
I wish
I had an extraordinary power
to turn your pain into self-acceptance.
I wish
I could anoint your hidden wounds
with a healing love
and help you make peace
with your past."
Look inside your heart
and make a promise,
"Dear heart,
I promise,

"I will not walk away from you.
I will always be here.
I will always help you heal.
I will pour my love into your wounds.
I will cover your scars with my devotion.
Don't be scared.
Nothing is more authentic than a love
that can heal.
I will be here.
This is my gift for you."

## Invisible Weapons

Nobody told you
that every virtue is
a transparent, shining armor
that protects you
during the wars of life.
Nobody told you
that every virtue is
an invisible, powerful weapon
that helps you fight
the battles of life.
Let love be your shield,
let prayer be your ammunition,
cover your soul
with wisdom,
and not a single cruel word
will ever harm you.
Wear the equipment of patience
and you will withstand
the cruel wars of life.
Put on the covering of kindness,

and nobody will be able to upset you.
Never take off the helmet of humility,
and arrogance will never suffocate you.
My friend,
protect your soul
under the armor of virtues
and go to these invisible wars
with bravery.

## Use Your Virtues

My friend,
your virtues are not abstract concepts.
You are a universe of energies,
and everything that comes out
from your soul
is alive.
Be aware of your powers,
for they hold positive energy.
You may ask yourself
where your strength comes from,
and I will tell you,
"Your strength comes from your virtues,"
so focus on them.
Multiply your virtues,
add more love to your generous soul,
be gentle and patient.
You will overcome your insecurities,
grow in love,
and reach inner peace.

## Your Inner World

The world is not made of
only what you see,
yet it is made of plenty of invisible things.
For example, faith.
Feelings.
Emotions.
Dreams.
Aspirations.
Every day is your time
to contribute to the beauty of the world
with the abundance of your faith,
with the treasure
of your beautiful feelings,
with the large spectrum
of your positive emotions
and aspirations.
My friend,
before adding your treasure
to the beauty of this world,
make your inner world

a place of positivity,
harmony,
peace,
kindness,
serenity,
calmness,
and love.
Transform your inner world
through healing.
It is an invisible work,
yet remember,
the world is not comprised of
only what you see.
It is made of
your spectacular inner world.
Take care of your little inner heaven.
This is your gift for this world.

## Something Beautiful

If you feel alone,
depressed,
or heartbroken,
then it is time
to rewrite your story.
Erase all toxic scars
from your past
with your tears.
Start healing your thoughts,
clean the dark walls
of your mind.
Journal something precious
about yourself
deep inside your heart.
Keep these affirmations
in your heart
like you would wear an amulet,
and fight every day
to become
what you have just written down.

## The Condition of a Child

If you want to heal your heart's wounds,
return to the condition of a child.
Recover the mind's purity
which only a child has.
Dress your heart in grace.
Forgive often,
but first,
forgive yourself.
Be meek and kind,
but first,
be meek and kind to yourself.
Discover small miracles
in everything around you,
but first,
discover a little miracle in your heart.
Cultivate resilience,
peace,
and serenity,
but first,
find something pure in your heart.

Make someone smile today,
but first,
make yourself smile.
Be gentle.
Show empathy
whenever you can,
but first,
show compassion to yourself.
Dream,
and be free in your dreams
like an eagle,
but never forget
to build the first dream for yourself.

## Your Dreams Matter

Even if you feel small right now,
be resilient
and cultivate your dreams.
You can't imagine
how much they matter in the long run.
Seed a dream in everything you do.
Nurture your aspirations
with meaningful beauty.
Dedicate time to dream,
to develop your values,
to have goals and ambitions,
and set noble expectations
for your life.
Don't spend a day
without dreaming.
That is what differentiates people.
Dream.
Cultivate your dreams.
No flower can live without roots.
Remind yourself

Alexandra Vasiliu

that your roots are your dreams –
the foundation of your soul,
the secret wings of your heart.
Water your roots every day.
Cultivate your dreams,
for in the long run,
your dreams will be all that matter.

## Prune Away

Prune away everything
that hinders your inner growth.
Prune away everything
that stops you from blooming.
Remind yourself,
your heart is a garden
filled with seeds of dreams
waiting to grow
and show their beauty.
Fight for your aspirations
and allow yourself to flourish.
Remind yourself,
you are meant
to bloom
and spread your inner beauty,
your unique way of loving.

## An Old Friend

Invite an old friend for a walk
and say,
"Let's take a walk in silence.
Hold my hand
and don't say a word.
Let's walk like children
who explore nature
and admire the silly shapes of clouds.
I need to walk with you in silence.
Then, if we sit down,
don't say anything.
Any comforting word you say
will invalidate my grief,
will make me feel bad.
Just sit down with me.
If I cry,
don't say anything.
Just cry with me.
Let our hearts find the best way to bond.
Be with me now.

"Be like a child with me,
for right now
I am like a vulnerable child,
in need of healing my broken heart.
Help me heal.
I need to return to simplicity."

I hope
your friend will respond,
"I will do everything
you asked me to do.
I want you to be healed.
Let's take a walk in silence.
We will say nothing,
while our hearts will share their secrets.
Healing is a miracle
created in silence and love.
Let's take a walk in silence.
We will find the answers within us."

## Words

As you grow,
you will realize
that there are words
that cut deeper than swords,
and words that frighten you
like rattlesnakes.
There are words
that scream in your head
at midnight,
and you have to wake up
and open the window of your soul
to let them out
as sighs and cries.
There are words
with sharp teeth
that bite your mind
like wild beasts.
And there are words
that can repair any broken heart.
Words that stitch,

bandage,
and anoint
the wounds of your heart.
Words that calm you down.
And words that heal.
Words that bring back to life
your dead soul.
Words that feed you with love
and succor you with drink
from the well of hope.
Words that cover you with joy.
Words that protect you
like a warm comforter.
And words that heal.
As you grow,
you will realize
that you are the master and the owner
of all these types of words.
It is up to you which ones you choose.
Don't play with your words,
for every word is a seed.
A seed of kindness
or a seed of hate.
It is up to you which you want to use,
for you become the image of the words
you have chosen.

## A Priceless Gem

Don't kill time,
for this is a priceless gem.
Time is God's gift,
so you can heal.
Make something beautiful
with every unique moment of your life.
Turn time into love.
Turn time into hope.
Turn every moment into a healing time.
Let kindness be your goal.
Do something unique with your heart.
Infuse it with beauty.
Aspire to love more,
and let kindness be your mission on earth.
These are the only ways
you will never waste the time of your life.
And you will heal.

## A Little Prayer

If you feel unloved,
unwanted,
unseen,
or unworthy,
draw a line in the sand.
You know
you can't continue like this.
"God,
please help me move on
and never step back behind this line.
Help me remember
that every moment is a moment
of healing,
growth,
and evolution.
Help me look deeper within,
discover my potential,
and believe in my strength."

## The Inward Journey

Time is not your enemy.
It is just the relationship
you build with yourself toward healing.
Nurture this relationship
with patience, wisdom, and grace,
and stay committed to healing yourself
no matter how long it takes.
This is your inward journey –
the most complicated
and essential journey of your life.
Stay humble
and take all the time in the world
to honor this journey.
Slide down inside your heart,
and pour self-forgiveness
into your wounds.
Healing is all about nurturing
your inner wounds
with love,
no matter how long it takes.

## You Have Everything

I know those scary feelings
when your mind is like a sieve,
and every thought is falling through it.
I know that terrifying emptiness
when you feel weird
like being in a parallel dimension.
I know
how it sounds
to scream inside your heart
and never receive an answer,
only a sad echo.
I know the heartbreaking feeling
of being crushed down
in millions of tiny pieces.
But my friend,
let me tell you
that I also have the determination
and the perseverance
to heal your wounds.
I also know

the resilience
and the inner strength
to become the best version of yourself.
I know
both sides of this recovery process.
And I know
that you do have everything you need
to heal,
rise,
grow,
love again,
and live beautifully.
You have everything.
Just be honest with yourself,
exit your inner chaos,
and find the path toward light.
This is the greatest gift
that you can give to yourself.

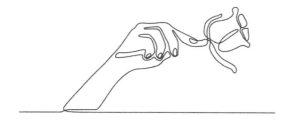

## The Anatomy of Self-Growth

The anatomy of self-growth
has five parts:
let go,
heal,
pray,
rise from ashes,
and move on.
The more you let go,
the more you heal.
The more you pray,
the higher you rise from ashes.
The more you do all these,
the less complicated
it will be
to move on.

## You Need A Map

Healing is a back-and-forth journey.
You travel
from your inner place of trauma
towards the fragile space of hope.
While you heal,
you build your identity map.
A map with millions of roads.
Some of them are long,
others are slippery,
and a few are dead-ends.
Be patient.
Trace your map with the hands of love.
Create this beautiful gift for yourself.
You are the first who can have
compassion and understanding
for yourself.
Be patient.
A map is essential
when you want
to move forward in life.

## Raise Your Voice

For so long,
you have been dogged by anxiety.
It is time to overcome your insecurities
and heal your soul.

Whenever you hear a voice telling you,
"You are not good at anything,"
give this response,
"I am good at learning
how to become a good person."
Whenever you hear your fears
raising their voices,
speak louder
and say to yourself,
"I am not scared.
God is my helper."

Be bold, gentle, and brave,
and build your identity
on love, clarity, and wisdom.

## No One

When I went through difficult times
in my life,
I wanted
to meet someone
who could give me
just a smidgen of hope,
"You will get out of depression,
no worries.
There is a new horizon
waiting for you,
therefore, be patient
and believe
in the gift of life."
But there was no one
who could give me
a kind, positive, healing word.
No one,
except for my soul
who kept whispering to me,
"You will get out of depression,

no worries.
"There is a new horizon
waiting for you,
therefore, be patient
and believe
in the gift of life."

This is why
when I went through difficult times
in my life,
I returned to myself.
My soul was the only supporter
that God gave me.

## Remember

In a time of affliction,
remember
that your soul was meant to be
a blooming flower.
In a time of sorrow,
remember
that your soul was created
with joy and light.
In a time of depression,
remember
that your soul craves
love, attention, and safety.
In a time of despair,
remember
that your soul was brought to life
in hope.
In a time of rejection,
remember
that you have roots in the sky.

## Never Alone

Take a short way back home,
back to yourself,
and seed these words
deep down into your heart,
*You are never alone.*
Look up to the sky,
there are millions of stars
spreading hope
every night.
Look up to the sky
and remind yourself,
*I am never alone.*

## Never Enough

You can never be enough for yourself.
People are social creatures
with innate emotional needs
and complex expectations,
and you are one of them.
You need to love
and be loved.
You need to forgive
and be forgiven.
You need to laugh
and dance.
You need to heal
and hope.
You need
to be generous
and dedicate yourself
to a noble goal.
You need to build dreams
with someone
and make plans for vacations.

You need to live in a wholesome way
and be happy.
For all these,
you need connections,
you need relationships,
you need souls around you.
Beautiful, brave, generous souls
like you.
Dare to accept
that you can never be enough for yourself.
You will free yourself from
what this tumultuous world says,
spreading empty words
and glittering statements.
You will understand
that being enough for yourself
is not the key
to an accomplished life.
You need others
to love,
to forgive,
to laugh with,
to dance,
to heal,
to learn generosity and dedication,
to build dreams with,
to make plans,

to live in a wholesome way,
and to be happy.
You see,
you can never be enough for yourself.
Be wise,
be strong,
and heal yourself
from this false teaching.
Your heart will be ready
for miracles,
because true love,
bright connections,
and healthy relationships
are the genuine blessings of your life.
And healing is a connective process.
A web of love will surround you.
Be wise,
be strong,
and never choose to be enough
for yourself.

## The Love You Deserve

Waiting for the love you deserve
will always mean a form of self-love,
a form of self-respect.
Be wise.
Respect yourself.
The love you deserve will come to you
and reveal the beauty of life.
Wait for this love.
Choose the one
with whom you can catch
beautiful dreams of happiness.
Wait –
this is the greatest gift
you can give to yourself
right now.

## Be Grateful

Dear woman,
be grateful
for your sensitive heart.
You are not a walking cage –
you are not only a body.
You are a unique home
for your beautiful soul.
From head to toe,
you are a sensitive, precious, bold soul.
A soul
who is singing,
dreaming,
filling the world
with her wonderful dreams.
Therefore, you are part of a minority –
you perceive the world
through the eyes of your heart.
You carry a sensitive heart,
so be grateful for this gift.

## The Only Thing

In the end,
it doesn't matter
how much you suffered,
how many losses
or rejections
you endured
in your life.
No, it doesn't matter.
You will never have to present
the catalog of your traumas.
Nobody is interested in
making an inventory
of your pains.
What matters the most
in this damaged world
is the ability
to turn your sufferings into kindness.
This is the only thing that matters.
This is the only thing
that people will notice about you

at first sight –
if you have become a healing soul
for everybody else.
My darling,
sufferings, rejections, losses
are common experiences
for all humans,
but very few of us
turn our woes into kindness
and refuse to become
bitter, hostile, or cruel.
So my darling,
in this damaged world,
value the ability
of turning pain into compassion.
Work on yourself.
Try to become a healing soul
for everybody else
around you.
One day,
this is the only thing that will remain.

## Hurt No Soul

Hurt no one.
Hurt no soul,
for every soul has untold stories
that are too painful to be shared.
Hurt no soul,
for every soul has hidden wounds
that never bleed.
Hurt no soul.
Hurt no one.
No matter how many difficulties
and sorrows
you have experienced,
try to hurt no one.
Be meek.
Be patient.
Be understanding.
Be empathetic.
Be gentle.
Be loving.
It is easy to be mean.

Anybody can be mean,
yet not everybody can be kind.
Differentiate yourself from the crowd.
Be kind.
Educate your heart to learn
the art of love
and kindness.
It takes courage and dignity
to have a good heart
amid the severe challenges of life.
Hurt no soul.
Be kind, my friend.

## The Book of Your Heart

Your heart is a book.
Every day,
you write the chapters of your life.
Try to make them bright
like the greatest poems
you have ever read.
Every day,
you can rewrite all the wrong chapters
of your life
and change them into beautiful poems.
Remind yourself,
every day,
you are the author of your life.

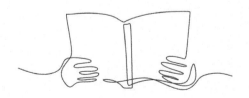

Everything that you do and say
is written in your heart.
The way you love and care,
the way you forgive and let go,
everything is written within you.
Your heart is a book.
Turn it into a healing book of love.
Live your life
in such a way
that people can say,
"Her life has been all love, not ego."
Live with dignity and generosity,
don't hurt anyone,
pray every day,
help others as much as you can.
Forgive often,
run away from hate and envy,
don't talk back or gossip,
heal other hearts with kindness,
and keep spreading love and purity
into this world of selfishness.
Live beautifully,
fill the book of your heart
with healing and poetry –
this is the greatest gift
that you can give to yourself
and to this world.

## Dear Reader,

Thank you very much for finding time to read my empowering poetry collection.

I hope that my poems helped you discover your unique beauty and renewed your faith in the healing power of love.

If so, please take a moment and show your appreciation by writing a short review on the website where you purchased this book. Your support means the world to me. Thank you.

With love and poetry,
Alexandra

# About the Author

Alexandra Vasiliu is an inspirational poet, and the bestselling author of *Healing Is a Gift, Healing Words, Time to Heal, Dare to Let Go*, and *Be My Moon*.

Alexandra double majored in Literature and French for her undergraduate degree before pursuing her Ph.D. in Medieval Literature. When she isn't busy writing, she can be found browsing in libraries and bookstores, outdoors chasing violet sunsets, or spending time with her family at the beach.

Get in touch with her on Instagram (@alexandravasiliupoetry) and Facebook (@AlexandraVasiliuWriter). Or visit her at alexandravasiliu.net. She loves hearing from her readers.